Finding Fossils

in the

Shark Tooth Capital

By

Judi Cobb

Judi Cobb

Illustrated by

Allison Daigle

Published by SunCoast Digital Press, Inc.

Introduction

Some years ago, I taught Second Grade in northwest Michigan. A Second Grade teacher from southwest Florida asked if our classes could become pen pals. We agreed. Next, our students mailed Petoskey stones with our letters to the Florida students. These stones contain fossils with six-sided coral shapes. They are found near Petoskey, Michigan, along the shores of Lake Michigan.

In return, the Florida students mailed letters to us along with prehistoric shark teeth. We were in awe and wanted to learn more about this fascinating subject.

Later on, my husband, Dick Cobb, joined a scuba dive charter off Venice Beach, Florida and discovered a six-inch prehistoric shark tooth, which is somewhat rare and valuable.

This brief book with photos and illustrations answers typical questions that would logically occur to a reader. I hope that this book will educate and inspire exploration.

Judi Cobb

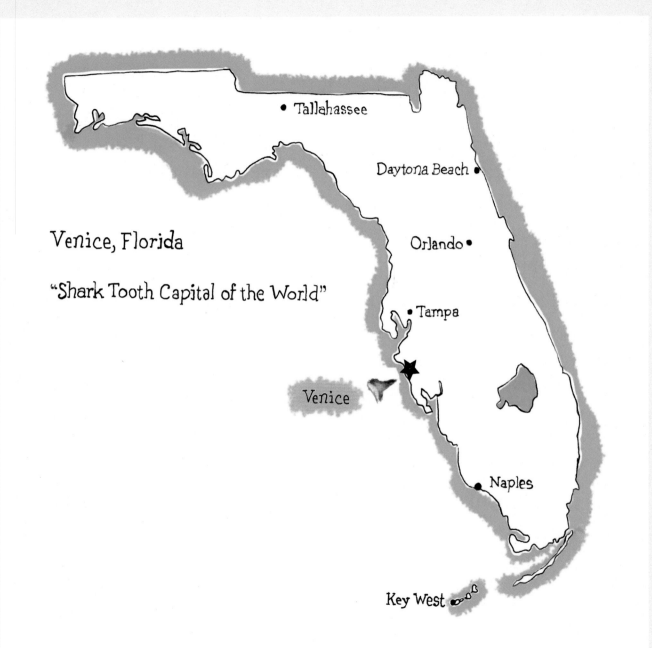

Venice, Florida

"Shark Tooth Capital of the World"

Shark Tooth Capital

Little gems slide through treasure hunters' fingers like polished jewels which have been buffed by a fine craftsman. The very feel of prehistoric shark teeth tends to soothe and delight the beachcombers in Venice, Florida.

This beautiful city in southwest Florida on the Gulf of Mexico is called the "Shark Tooth Capital of the World." People find thousands of prehistoric shark teeth here.

Prehistoric means long ago, before people recorded history. Those who walk the beaches find shark teeth which are over a million years old. Teeth from living sharks are white. Not many of these are found.

Prehistoric teeth are no longer white. They become brown, gray, or black and have become fossils. A *fossil* is any remains of an animal or plant from a thousand or more years ago, which has turned to stone. The color of a fossil can fool people. It does not always explain how old the item is.

Instead, it can mean that the shark tooth or other fossil became colored like the sand, mud or other sediment that it had been buried in. *Sediment* (SED-uh-munt) means dirt, rock or sand that has been moved to a place by ice, water or wind.

Many beachgoers simply pick up teeth by hand. Others use a long-handled wire basket, available in local stores. The fossil hunters lower the basket in shallow water and pull it along the sandy bottom. Next, they raise their shovel to examine prehistoric shark teeth, shells, and other treasures.

The Venice Shark Tooth Festival is held yearly to celebrate the area's fossilized shark teeth. Each April, this event features fossil vendors, arts and crafts, entertainment, education booths, and food. People may purchase teeth at the festival or shop for them in nearby stores.

Shark teeth can be found in other temperate (mild) and tropical (warm) water locations in the United States and the rest of the world. But for some reason, Venice, Florida, has an abundance of them.

There are 350 or more species of living sharks. *Species* means a group of living things whose members are closely related. Some of the kinds of shark teeth found on Venice beaches include: bull, dusky, lemon, mako, sand, tiger, white tip, and others.

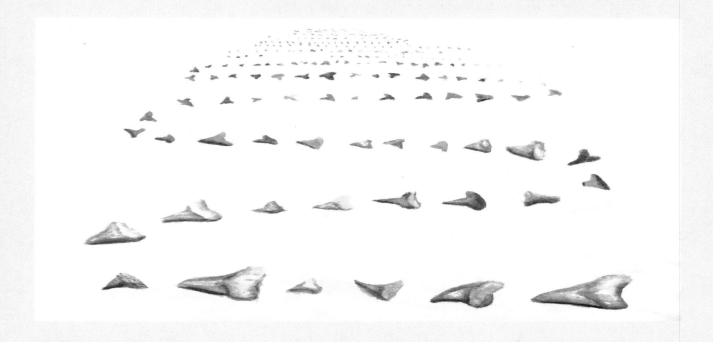

Sharks have as many as 250 teeth growing in rows called *files*. As they lose a tooth, another one moves forward. These fish shed their teeth as easily as a dog sheds fur. Then more and more teeth are produced. It is possible for a single shark to lose up to 24,000 teeth or more in a lifetime! Since millions of sharks have lived over millions of years, there is a bountiful supply of teeth to be found.

Mega Treasure

Some lucky hunters get to find a specimen from the largest prehistoric shark ever — the Carcharodon *Megalodon* (kar-char-o-don MEG-a-lo-don).

Some scientists want to call it *Carcharocles* (kar-Char-o-kleys) because experts disagree on whether this fish was related to the great white shark. Either name can be hard to pronounce, so we will call it "C. Meg."

This extinct shark was about 60 feet long. That is larger than a school bus or about the size of ten tall men, placed end to end.

Did you know that *mega* is a word part which means *great* or *immense*?

Teeth from a C. Meg have been found up to 7 inches long! A modern great white shark's teeth can be up to 3 inches long, while most shark teeth are much smaller.

On a C. Meg with a total length of 52 feet, the first dorsal fin (on the back) would be taller than an average woman. The pectoral fins (on each side of the chest) would each be the length of a 10-foot ladder. A C. Meg's tail would be taller than a 6-foot man standing on the shoulders of another 6-foot man!

This photograph shows the author's husband,
a scuba diver, holding a huge 6-inch long C. Meg
tooth that he found.

He discovered it off Venice Beach in about 20 feet of water. Mr. Cobb traveled about one mile from shore in a dive charter boat.

He gently fanned the ocean bottom until he felt something shaped like a triangle. The Dive Master and other divers were very excited about Mr. Cobb's find for the day!

This photo on the left shows a portion of the author's shark tooth collection. All it takes is a visit to Venice, Florida, the Shark Tooth Capital of the World, to start your own collection.

This fossil is thought to be over 15 million years old! Scientists think that no living shark today has teeth this big.

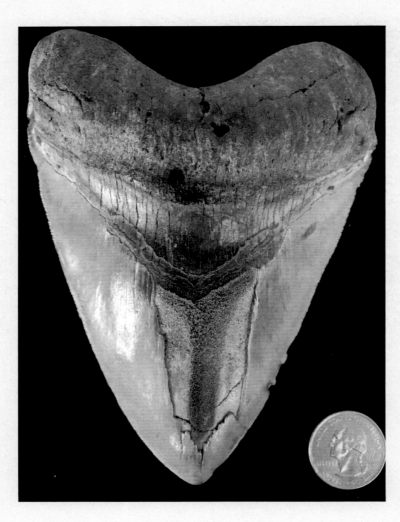

It helps to know that Florida used to be under the sea until about 10,000 years ago (or more). This explains why shark teeth can be found even in fresh water locations, where you may not expect to find them.

Venice Beach, the Shark Tooth Capital, is not the only place to find these little treasures. You can also look for these fossils at Caspersen Beach, just south of Venice Beach, and at several other nearby beaches and rivers. Surprisingly, you can even find them inland in rivers and springs.

In fact, visitors to Disney World may consider taking a side trip to Kelly Park, a State Park near Orlando. A certain tributary (branch) of the Wekiva River is called Rock Springs, where fresh spring water spouts from openings in rock. This stream forms other little side creeks and pools.

Visitors, ready to explore, have found buried shark teeth near little pop-up springs in these areas. How fascinating to find shark teeth in the fresh, natural flowing water of Rock Springs. This reminds us that Florida really had been covered by ocean water many, many years ago.

C. Meg teeth have been found throughout Florida and in Alabama, California, Georgia, Maryland, New Jersey, North Carolina, South Carolina, and Virginia.

Worldwide, these teeth have been discovered in Africa, Asia, Australia, Europe, and South America.

This impressive C. Meg jaw belongs to the former owner of Florida West SCUBA & CHARTERS and is no longer on display.

Experts try to learn as much as they can from shark teeth because they have little else to go on. Unlike some fish and mammals, which die and sometimes float to shore, C. Meg's skeleton was made of *cartilage* (like we have inside our nose and ears), not bone. Most cartilage dissolves in seawater.

After other fish feed on a dead shark, very little is left except for its teeth which sink to the ocean floor to become fossils. Shark teeth are made of *dentin* (a hard, calcified tissue) which does not easily break down. In fact, the dentin is even harder than bone because it is covered with a very hard enamel surface.

Later on, storm action may move the sand around and allow the teeth to be washed to the shore in the waves.

C. Meg may have been a shallow water predator. A *predator* (PRED-a-tor) is an animal that kills other animals for food. Scientists have found whale bones with teeth marks from C. Meg.

The edges of C. Meg's teeth were serrated with zigzags like a saw or a steak knife. This allowed the fish's bite to cut right through the bone.

Chances are that C. Meg ate whales, seals, sea lions, dolphins and other large fish.

Let's Compare

People believe that C. Meg was about as ferocious as the dinosaur, Tyrannosaurus Rex. T. Rex, a terrestrial predator, grew to about 50 feet tall. Some teeth were up to 12 inches long. We no longer have creatures quite like that!

The whale shark is the largest fish in the world now. (It's not really a whale.) This fish can grow up to about 56 feet long. It is a gentle shark with tiny teeth. It lives near the equator and eats plankton and small fish. *Plankton* means little animals and plant life which drift in the water.

The great white shark seems to be the most feared aquatic creature nowadays. It can grow to be 30 feet long. The great white shark's serrated teeth range from 2 to 3 inches long.

A great white shark does NOT hunt people for food, but sometimes does harm them. A shark can mistake a person for another animal, such as a sea lion.

It is quite safe to swim in supervised areas of the ocean, with others.

Avoid places where sharks are known to feed.

Thankfully, the largest prehistoric shark ever, C. Meg, poses no threat to us today. It is fortunate that there are exciting facts to be learned and mega teeth to be found, two million years after this shark became extinct.

Like its larger relative, C. Meg, today's Great White Shark preys on seals.

Glossary

Aquatic (a-KWAT-ik) of the water, living in the water. A shark is aquatic.

Carcharodon Megalodon (kar-CHAR-o-din MEG-a-lo-don) scientific name for a certain large extinct shark thought to be related to the great white shark.

Carcharocles (kar-CHAR-a-kleys) scientific name for the same large extinct shark. Named differently by those who believe the great white shark is unrelated.

Cartilage (Kar-tel-lij) a flexible skeleton, not of bone.

Extinct (IK-stingkt) died out, the end of a species.

Ferocious (FERO-shes) violent, fierce, wild.

Fossil (FOS-el) any hard remains of an animal or plant from over 1,000 years ago which has been buried in protective sediment.

Glossary

Mammals (MA-muhls) animals which produce milk for their young and have fur or hair.

Marine (ME-ren) Aquatic.

Migrate (MY-grate) to move from one place to another. Some sharks move to warmer waters when the seasons change.

Plankton (PLANK-ton) little animal and plant life which drift in the water.

Predator (PRED-a-tor) an animal which hunts other animals for food.

Prehistoric (PRE-his-torik) long ago before people recorded history in written form.

Shallow (SHAL-oh) not deep.

Glossary

Sediment (Sed-uh-munt) dirt, rock or sand moved to a place by ice, water, or wind.

Serrated (SER-rat-ed) sharp, notched edges.

Species (SPEE-sheez) a group of living things, whose members are closely related.

Temperate (TEM-pur-it) places or oceans not too hot or too cold.

Threat (thret) possible harm.

Tropical (TROP-ik-il) describes area close to equator where the sun is strongest. Hot place or warm ocean. (Subtropical describes warm area between temperate and tropical zones).

Acknowledgments

I wish to thank my publisher, Barbara Dee of Suncoast Digital Press, Inc., who provided encouragement and who enlightened me about finding shark teeth in the unusual area of a natural springs—Rock Springs in Apopka, Florida near Orlando.

I am also thankful to my late husband, Dick Cobb, who discovered a mega shark tooth, which delighted him and which spurred my interest in writing this book.

Thanks go out to Florida West SCUBA & CHARTERS of Venice, Florida for their role in providing the dive charter for Mr. Cobb.

I am very grateful to Marge Ellis whose class became pen pals with my class so many years ago and who first introduced us to the idea of finding prehistoric shark teeth.

I was very fortunate to have the support of my daughters, Renee Cobb and Shelly Kennedy. I am especially grateful to Renee who helped to type this manuscript.

Florida West SCUBA & CHARTERS

www.megalodoncharters.com

About the Author

Judi Cobb, author and retired teacher, became intrigued with the study of shark teeth when her Michigan class of second-grade students received a supply of prehistoric shark teeth, and even more so when her husband gifted her with a giant, multi-million year old tooth he found while scuba diving near their home in Florida.

A lifelong learner, she decided to do her own research into shark teeth, just for fun! Reflecting on how much children love to learn about natural wonders, she decided to write Finding Fossils in the *Shark Tooth Capital*. The major portion of her teaching career was devoted to early elementary education, though she was called on to teach every grade and subject, from kindergarten through twelfth grades.

Cobb holds a B.A. from Eastern Michigan University, and pursued graduate studies in Elementary Education at Michigan State University. Her career also includes service to children as a Case Manager and Child Custody Investigator for the 13th Circuit Court of Michigan.

Originally from Traverse City, Michigan, she now resides on the West Coast of Florida, not too far from Venice Beach, the "Shark Tooth Capital of the World." She is very active in her community, and also enjoys visits from her grandchildren, Finn Kennedy and Loch Kennedy, who live in Madison, Wisconsin.

51751557R00024

Made in the USA
Columbia, SC
23 February 2019